Original title:
Fables of Fir and Fun

Copyright © 2025 Creative Arts Management OÜ
All rights reserved.

Author: Beckett Sinclair
ISBN HARDBACK: 978-1-80567-378-1
ISBN PAPERBACK: 978-1-80567-677-5

The Whispering Woods

In the woods where the trees gossip,
Squirrels practice their acorn toss,
The rabbits giggle at the mishaps,
While the wise old owl just scoffs.

A raccoon juggles pine cones with flair,
Singing songs that fill the air,
The brook chuckles, splashes in play,
As shadows dance and sway all day.

The wind carries tales of the night,
Of foxes who dance under pale moonlight,
With each rustle, laughter draws near,
For mischief thrives, that much is clear.

So if you wander, take care to hear,
The whispers of joy that bring good cheer,
In this woodland filled with giggles and fun,
Where every twig knows how to run.

Legacy of the Luminous Leaves

Beneath the boughs of glittering green,
The leaves share secrets rarely seen,
Frogs compete in a leap and a hop,
While mischievous bugs play hide and stop.

A chameleon boasts of its bright hue,
While sloths hang low, enjoying the view,
Each colorful tale, a humorous lore,
Echoes through branches, ever more.

At night, the fireflies start their ballet,
Lighting up paths for the creatures at play,
Each flicker a spark of laughter and jest,
In this kingdom of joy, no critter can rest.

So dance with the leaves, let spirits soar,
For life's just a game—nothing less, nothing more,
In the canopy where giggles revive,
A legacy thrives, as all come alive.

The Festival of Forest Friends

Gather 'round for a wacky parade,
Where creatures unite in grand masquerade,
Bunnies with hats, and foxes in ties,
Dance on the grass beneath sunny skies.

Squirrels spin tales over peanut dishes,
While porcupines grant their prickly wishes,
The badgers play drums made from logs,
While owls hoot along, oh what a slog!

Each step is a slip, each twirl is a trip,
From the elder tree's grand, leafy tip,
Raccoons and deer join in without care,
Roaring with laughs that fill up the air.

So come one, come all, to this festive spree,
Where nature's harmony sings in glee,
For in this merry gathering's embrace,
Every friend is welcomed, every smile a trace.

Enchantment by the Emerald Stream

Beside the stream, where froggies croak,
The fish make faces, a real funny joke,
With each little splash, the sunbeams play,
Whirling around in a splashy ballet.

Beetles in suits lead a parade of glee,
As dragonflies buzz in wild jubilee,
The laughter of crickets fills the calm air,
With every note, there's a dance to share.

The reeds sway gently, tall and proud,
While a turtle tries to sing out loud,
But all it gets is a burbling song,
As the ants march by, all together throng.

In this realm where the silly reign,
With each little blunder, joy is the gain,
So dip your toes in, let the fun beam,
And lose yourself by the emerald stream.

The Starlit Stump

Upon a stump so tall and wide,
A raccoon danced with panda pride.
The fireflies blinked, a playful crowd,
While owls hooted, oh so loud.

They twirled and spun in a merry way,
Chasing shadows until the break of day.
The moon chuckled, her silver light,
Watched the critters laugh with delight.

A squirrel juggled acorns quite high,
While hedgehogs cheered, oh me, oh my!
With every tumble and every fall,
The stump echoed their joyous call.

When morning came, they waved goodbye,
The starlit stump, a memory nigh.
In dreams they'd dance when night would fall,
Forever bound by laughter's call.

Tales of the Mischievous Mice

In a cupboard beneath the stairs,
Mice held parties without any cares.
Cheese was served on a silver plate,
While the cat snoozed, they'd celebrate!

With tiny hats and a toast so grand,
They danced in circles, paw in hand.
The crumbs of cake rained like snow,
As giggles echoed, "Oh, let's go!"

They played hide and seek with bits of cheese,
Nibbled slippers with the greatest ease.
A ruckus arose, a squeak and a shout,
As the cat woke up, and they quickly sprouted!

Under the floorboards, they squeaked in fright,
"Did you hear that? Let's hide for the night!"
With laughter shared in the dark, you'd find,
Mischievous mice, with hearts intertwined.

The Cricket's Serenade

At dusk when shadows softly creep,
A cricket chirped while others sleep.
His tiny voice, a charming tune,
Brought stars to dance beneath the moon.

"Dear ladybugs, come join my song!
Let's frolic here where we belong!
The night is young, and so we'll sing,
With all the joy that nature brings."

The frogs joined in, a chorus bold,
Their croaks a story, humor untold.
A bullfrog leapt, a funny sight,
Landed near with a splash of light.

With every note, the world felt right,
Nature chuckled, bathing in light.
The cricket bowed, his serenade,
A memory made that would never fade.

The Harmony of Hoots

Under the trees where the night winds blow,
Owl family gathers in a row.
They share their tales with flair and style,
Hooting stories that make you smile.

"Once I spotted a mouse on a hill,
Thought I'd catch him, but slipped—what a thrill!"
The youngest owl giggled with glee,
"Tell us again, oh crafty spree!"

With wisdom wrapped in guffaws and sighs,
The night air filled with playful cries.
With each hoot, the laughter grew,
In the woods where dreams feel new.

As dawn approached, the stars grew meek,
Yet their laughter echoed, never weak.
In the harmony of hoots, they found,
A bond of joy that knows no bound.

The Foxglove's Secret

In a garden bright, with colors bold,
The foxglove whispers, tales untold.
Bees wear tiny hats, buzzing away,
While tulips dance, in the sun's warm ray.

A secret party, with tea and cakes,
Where hedgehogs giggle and nobody wakes.
The daisies join, in a wiggly line,
As butterflies twirl, sipping nectar fine.

Squirrels play cards, with acorns as chips,
While laughter erupts, from tiny critter lips.
The moon peeks in, at this crazy scene,
With stars on the side, like a fairy queen.

Adventures Beneath the Canopy

Beneath the broad and leafy dome,
A troupe of creatures call it home.
Chirping frogs and giggling mice,
Plan their outings, oh so nice.

The raccoon dons a pirate hat,
While toads spin tales with a mighty spat.
A game of tag amongst the trees,
As squirrels leap with joyful ease.

A treasure map, sketched in the dirt,
Leads to a prize, a big red shirt.
With playful shouts, they search around,
Finding giggles instead, from the ground.

The Whimsical Wind

The wind had mischief on its mind,
Whirling leaves, all twirled and entwined.
A top hat flew from a gopher's head,
Through the trees, it joyfully sped.

Dancing branches swayed to and fro,
As the wind beckoned, 'Come on, let's go!'
The pine trees laughed, with a rustling cheer,
Shaking their needles, spreading good cheer.

A gusty giggle, a playful twist,
Knocking over acorns, not one was missed.
All critters joined, in a frolicsome spree,
Chasing the wind, as happy as can be.

The Badger and the Midnight Feast

In the heart of the woods, when the moon's up high,
A badger invited the friends nearby.
"Bring your best snacks!" he called out loud,
"A feast awaits, for a hungry crowd!"

With carrots and cakes, they all set the scene,
A table of treats, oh so fit for a queen.
The owls brought pastries, the mice had cheese,
While rabbits jumped in, to say, "More, please!"

They dined and laughed, until morning's light,
Sharing their stories, what a delight!
But as dawn approached, they knew the score,
Had to hurry home, or they'd snore for sure.

The Enchanted Forest Chronicles

In a forest full of chatter,
Squirrels dance, oh, what a clatter!
Trees in love with songbirds' tunes,
Mischief thrives beneath the moons.

A fox wearing shoes made of leaves,
Told the owl, "You won't believe!"
They played tag with a rabbit bright,
Who hopped in shadows, out of sight.

Bumbling bears with hats askew,
Join the party, join the crew!
With giant mushrooms as their stage,
They twirl and leap, the life of page.

A snail sliding with quite the flair,
Said, "I'll race you to who knows where!"
But surprising laughter fills the air,
As everyone trips, landing with care.

Creatures of the Hidden Glade

Beneath the boughs where secrets play,
Get ready for a wild display!
A hedgehog juggles acorns round,
While frogs leap up, they're glory-bound.

A raccoon with a monocle neat,
Debates with badgers, quite a feat!
They argue over berries sweet,
While ladybugs tap tiny feet.

Lively critters paint the leaves,
With colors bright that one believes,
The trees start giggling, what a scene,
As chipmunks act like a queen bee.

Tales told in whispers, soft and low,
Where laughter blooms like flowers grow,
The hidden glade's a quirky place,
With every twist, joy takes its space.

Laughter Among the Pines

When pine trees sway in gentle breeze,
All creatures gather with such ease.
The crows crack jokes and knack their beaks,
While porcupines share silly squeaks.

A parrot dressed in polka dots,
Chirps out riddles, like it or not!
The squirrels munch on popcorn treats,
As laughter echoes, joy repeats.

Bees buzz in on secret plans,
To throw a dance—and oh, those spans!
With moonlight shining, shadows prance,
Who knew the woods could host a dance?

At midnight's peak, the laughter swells,
In stories spun, every heart dwells,
Among the pines, a light so bright,
With funny wonders, pure delight.

The Pine Cone's Secret Adventure

A pine cone rolled down the hill,
Said, "Adventure waits, if you will!"
With twigs as friends, it bounced and danced,
Across the stream, all trees were pranced.

A chipmunk joined with nuts in hand,
"Let's explore this merry land!"
They found a hat from last year's fair,
And wore it proudly, without a care.

Through meadows where the daisies play,
They laughed and sang the whole day away.
But oh, the squirrel with stealthy paws,
Stole their hats with little applause!

In silly chases 'neath the skies,
The pine cone laughed, no need for sighs.
For every tumble, every fall,
Was part of joy, the best of all.

Dances of the Dappled Light

In the woods where shadows play,
A squirrel swayed in grand ballet.
With acorn hats, they took the stage,
Chasing sunbeams, setting the gauge.

A rabbit twirled with such delight,
Underneath the giggling light.
They spun and hopped, all in a rush,
While wildflowers cheered, in a hush.

A fox joined in, with winks and grins,
Prancing about, he just can't win.
Each step a slip on leafy ground,
A comic scene, so joyfully found.

As laughter echoed through the trees,
Nature joined in, swaying with ease.
The dappled light danced with the crew,
In a festival, fresh and new.

The Curious Case of the Bark-Bound Tome

In an oak, a book was trapped tight,
Filled with tales to spark delight.
Its pages crinkled, full of mischief,
Adventures bold, and moments brisk.

A raccoon peeked, with eyes so wide,
"How to escape?" he gently cried.
He pulled and tugged, with little grace,
Till the book sprang forth from its place.

Birds gathered round, all eager to see,
What secrets lay, wild and free.
The pages fluttered, tales galore,
Of drinks spilled, and shoes left at the door.

Each word a giggle, every line a spree,
The characters danced, happy as can be.
They vowed to rebind, in laughter's embrace,
And carry their fables all over the place.

Tales from the Twisted Trunks

In a grove with trunks all twisted,
A rumor grew, hilariously insisted.
"See that branch? It tickles the skies!"
"Oh, how it giggles!" the owl replies.

They say the trees gossip like old pals,
Swapping stories of woodland gals.
With tales of rabbits and mischievous bees,
And deep in the hollow, a laughing breeze.

One trunk told of a bear's fancy feast,
Who donned a top hat for an antique beast.
Chasing his tail, he spun around,
And down came the honey, laughter abound.

With each twist and turn, stories arose,
Filling the air with joyous echoes.
In the heart of the grove, laughter rings true,
As trees share their secrets, just for a view.

Revelry in the Rooted Realm

Down in the roots where chaos swells,
Creatures gather with giggles and yells.
A toad in a hat holds a curious dance,
As the mushrooms clap, giving a chance.

The hedgehogs roll with plumes of cheer,
Bouncing about, their spines sincere.
With a skip and a hop, they form a line,
In the rooted realm, everything's fine.

The fireflies spark in rhythm and light,
Creating a show that lasts through the night.
Whispers of laughter fill up the glade,
As everyone joins in the revelry parade.

From the grassy floor to the storied boughs,
Joy overflows, so raise up your brows!
In the rooted realm, they dance and prance,
A woodland party, a wild expanse.

The Laughing Leaves of Lore

In the forest where giggles grow,
Leaves quiver with tales they know.
Squirrels spin stories, wild and bold,
Of acorns and mischief, all retold.

A fox in a hat did dance and prance,
While rabbits snickered, caught in the chance.
With every rustling, laughter flows,
A symphony of joy that grows!

The sunbeams tickle the bark of the trees,
As shadows join in, swaying with ease.
Mice in the meadow munch on their seeds,
Whispering jingles, fulfilling their needs.

With a clap of thunder, the fun ignites,
As bugs join in with their tiny delights.
In this merry glade, under skies so clear,
The laughing leaves echo far and near.

Whimsy Wrapped in Wildwood

In every twist of the winding trail,
A jolly sprite tells a cheeky tale.
Branches wave as if to say,
Come dance with us, don't stay away!

Bees wear stripes as they hum their tune,
While frogs in tuxedos croak at the moon.
The dew-drops giggle, bright and spry,
As butterflies hitch a comedic fly.

Charming critters in a game so grand,
Playing hopscotch on soft, golden sand.
With leafy confetti, they cheer and spin,
In wildwood's embrace, the joy is within.

For every rustle, there's laughter near,
As the trees join in with a hearty cheer.
Around every corner, the whimsy calls,
In the wildwood's heart, laughter enthralls.

Whispers of the Woodland

The winds carry whispers through branches high,
A chuckle here, a giggle nigh.
Mischievous critters play hide and seek,
With cheeky grins, not a hint of meek.

The owls hoot jokes that make you snort,
While raccoons plot a playful retort.
In the shade of the trees, the tales arise,
With every twinkle, a laughter surprise.

A dancing leaf twirls on a breeze,
Making friends with the buzzing bees.
Each sound a note in the woodland play,
A concert of chuckles that brightens the day.

And as dusk falls, the lanterns glow,
The woodland whispers softer, slow.
Yet in the twilight, echoes remain,
Of joyous laughter, clear as the rain.

The Tale of the Singing Stones

Once upon a time, by a babbling brook,
Stones gathered round, each one a book.
With voices like pebbles, they sang in tune,
A melody sweet as a bright afternoon.

They sang of the breeze that tickled their sides,
And the moon that danced with the night-time tides.
Each verse was a giggle, a spark of delight,
Bringing laughter and joy to the soft twilight.

A turtle tapped rhythm, a worm wiggled near,
All joined the chorus, no trace of fear.
The crickets accompanied with their own sparks,
Creating a symphony, lighting the dark.

As dawn broke the silence, their song took flight,
Carrying giggles to the sky, oh so bright.
And though they are stones, with hearts made of cheer,
The tale of their singing, we hold ever dear.

Magic in the Maple's Heart

In the tree where giggles bloom,
A squirrel wears a tiny costume.
With acorns stacked like little hats,
He dances round with chubby rats.

The branches sway like happy teens,
Telling tales of maple dreams.
The wind brings laughter, soft and sweet,
As critters gather for a treat.

A robin spins a magic tale,
Of feathered friends who sail and sail.
With every flap, a joke takes flight,
As daylight fades to warm moonlight.

In the heart of this leafy realm,
A world of joy and fun at the helm.
Let's join the cheer, the sweet old art,
And find the magic in the heart.

The Journey of the Wandering Breeze

The breeze sets off with mischief planned,
Tickling leaves, it swirls and stands.
It whispers secrets to each tree,
Then laughs and dances wild and free.

It blows a hat off Mr. Bee,
Who buzzes off with utmost glee.
A riddle tossed to kindly blooms,
As laughter echoes through the rooms.

Through fields it rushes, singing loud,
Making ripples in the crowd.
Each step a giggle, every swirl,
A fleeting chase in nature's whirl.

So let the breeze take joyous flight,
With every turn, it brings delight.
For in its journey, fun is found,
In every nook, laughter resounds.

Stories Under the Starry Sky

Beneath the stars, the critters meet,
Sharing tales that can't be beat.
A bunny hops and starts to mime,
Each story tickles, every time.

A turtle brings his sleepy grin,
While fireflies dance, the night begins.
With every flicker, a joke appears,
As chuckles bubble like bright cheers.

The owls hoot jokes, wise and sly,
Leaving all the frogs to sigh.
With laughter echoing through the night,
Each star above shines pure delight.

In this cozy, twinkling place,
Friends share wisdom with a face.
For in the night, when shadows play,
The stories light the starry way.

The Dancing Leaves

The leaves are swirling all around,
In a frolicsome, whirling sound.
With colors bright, they sway and spin,
Like dancers waiting to begin.

A gust of wind, a playful tease,
Turns trees into wobbly knees.
They giggle loud, they twist and clap,
While nature takes a happy nap.

A leaf named Larry leaps with glee,
He loves the stage, oh can't you see?
With every twirl and flutter bold,
He spins his tales—his laughter gold.

So come and join this leafy show,
Find joy in every little blow.
For in their dance, a lesson starts—
Life is better with funny hearts.

Stories from the Heart of the Forest

In the glade where whispers play,
A squirrel juggled nuts all day.
He slipped and spun, a comic sight,
As branches danced in dappled light.

The owl with glasses, wise and round,
Made jokes that echoed through the ground.
The rabbits laughed till bellies ached,
In every riddle, giggles baked.

Underneath the starry sky,
The fox would tell a tale or lie.
'Twas purest mischief every night,
As fireflies glimmered, oh so bright.

With every giggle, shadows play,
In woods where magic finds its way.
They weave a tapestry of delight,
In stories spun till morning light.

The Jests of the Woodland Court

In a clearing where critters convene,
The badger wears a crown quite green.
With humor sharper than his claws,
He stands to jest, and all applaud.

The hedgehog jokes, his quills askew,
Telling tales of things he'd do.
The laughter spreads, a joyful sound,
As woodland folk gather around.

A turtle slow, he tells his dream,
Of racing fast—oh, what a scheme!
The crowd erupts in wild delight,
His little legs, such a funny sight!

Now forest friends, so full of cheer,
In every jest, they shed a tear.
With every laugh, new bonds they form,
In this grand court, a spirit warm.

Harmony in the Hush of Trees

In the canopy where whispers blend,
The breeze brings joy, a gentle friend.
The leaves all giggle, shaking free,
As critters dance with carefree glee.

A chattering chipmunk finds a tune,
That makes the moonlight tap and swoon.
With silly hops and spins so grand,
He leads the fun, a merry band.

The stars above, they twinkle bright,
As laughter fills the peaceful night.
Each creature joins the playful song,
A harmony that feels so strong.

With every rustle, laughter soars,
In the hush of trees, it gently roars.
The heart of night, a playful dwell,
Where joy and friendship always swell.

The Sprite's Silly Serenade

In twilight's arms, a sprite took flight,
With laughter crisp and wings of light.
She tickled flowers, made them giggle,
As moonbeams joined her frolic, wiggle!

Her song, a tune of clumsy cheer,
Brought critters dancing far and near.
The toads croaked loud, the beetles drummed,
In this wild show, all hearts succumbed.

With every note, they'd laugh and spin,
As nature joined, a merry din.
The night unfolded, joyful spree,
In the sprite's dance among the trees.

So if you hear a chime at dusk,
A melody wrapped in nature's husk,
Know it's the sprite with laughter free,
Inviting all to share her glee.

Fantasies of Frosted Foliage

In the woods where whispers play,
Leaves giggle in disarray.
Snowflakes dance on branches high,
Frosty hats on trees, oh my!

Squirrels wear their winter coats,
While rabbits float on icy boats.
A clumsy moose on frozen ground,
Trips on twigs with a thud and sound.

Pinecones roll in laughter low,
Tickling foxes as they go.
A chilly breeze brings squeaky laughs,
As nature plays its wacky gaffs.

By the brook where snowflakes swirl,
Laughter from each critter's twirl.
The frost may chill, but spirits soar,
In this space where fun's in store!

The Daring Quest for Sunbeams

A brave little mouse sets out with glee,
Chasing sunbeams, oh so free!
With a map made of crayon bright,
He scurries fast, what a sight!

Squirrels cheer from heights above,
Singing songs of friendship and love.
Unicorns dance on a rainbow's tail,
While the mouse tells his wondrous tale.

Through fields of daisies, past the stream,
Every turn sparks a new dream.
A hidden spot with the purest light,
The mouse squeaks, "Adventure feels just right!"

With giggles ringing through the air,
He meets friends who simply care.
In the quest for warmth and bliss,
He finds more magic than he could miss!

Secrets of the Sylvan Realm

In the hush of leaves so bright,
Whispers fill the gentle night.
Owl and hedgehog share a joke,
While shadows dance and moonbeams poke.

Behind each trunk and leafy space,
Are giggling fairies in a race.
With flickering lights, they play a game,
Making the stars feel a bit lame.

The secrets of the forest roar,
As each creature finds their score.
Bats in capes and moles in hats,
Do the silly side-step with the rats.

As the night drifts into dreams,
The woodland hums with perfect themes.
In this realm of laughter bright,
Where every dusk brings pure delight!

The Legend of the Lost Birch

Once stood a birch, stately and grand,
With secrets hidden in its band.
One day it swore to take a break,
And went to dance by the shimmering lake.

The squirrels gasped, "Where could she go?"
While frogs croaked songs, putting on a show.
The birch spun round with a twinkle of fun,
As ripples shimmered under the sun.

The forest searched from dusk till dawn,
With rabbit footprints stretching far and long.
"I'll find my friend!" chirped a bold little crow,
"Even if it means I must go slow!"

At last, they found her twirling bright,
Folly and laughter painting the night.
Together they danced 'neath the moon's sweet watch,
To the rhythm of joy, they swayed and swatched!

The Guardian of the Glade

In the heart of the woods, where the laughter gleams,
A guardian stands, wrapped in leafy dreams.
With a hat made of flowers and shoes of bright bark,
He dances with squirrels from dawn until dark.

The creatures all giggle, they gather around,
As he juggles with acorns and leaps off the ground.
A tumble, a roll, then a grand, goofy bow,
In the kingdom of green, he reigns with a vow.

But one day a fox, a trickster so sly,
Planned to swindle the glade with a quick little lie.
"Your hat's not a flower, but a cabbage instead!"
The guardian chuckled, "At least it's well-fed!"

So they danced all together, no worries or cares,
The glade full of laughter, the joys they all share.
With a wink and a grin, the trickster soon learned,
That love and good humor are what he had yearned.

Tales Written in Petals

Among blossoms so bright, stories twist and twine,
Each petal a tale, each stem a fine line.
A rose told a secret to a daisy so fair,
While thistles joined in, with quite the flair.

"Once lived a snail, slow and grand," said the rose,
"He challenged a rabbit, as legend goes!"
The daisies all giggled, the thistles laughed loud,
As tales intertwined, a soft, flowery crowd.

Then took flight a bee, buzzing with glee,
"I heard a new tale, do listen to me!"
He spun a fine yarn of a butterfly's chase,
Who danced on the breeze, through the same sunny space.

The petals were shaking, in mirth they did sway,
As each story bloomed, brightening the day.
So gather the flowers, hold tales in your heart,
In gardens of laughter, it's where we'll not part.

The Song of the Silver Stream

Down in the valley, where waters do gleam,
A silver stream sings, in melody and dream.
With bubbles that giggle and ripples that play,
It tickles the rocks, brightening each day.

The fish join the chorus, a splashy parade,
While frogs croak along, in a tuneful charade.
A turtle on a log keeps tempo with ease,
As birds chirp high, rustling leaves in the breeze.

But a grumpy old bear, on the bank all alone,
Declared, "I can't stand this lonesome tone!"
The fish rolled their eyes, the frogs coughed a laugh,
"Join us, dear bear, we'll split things in half!"

So the bear took a plunge, into laughter and cheer,
Splashing water high, overcoming his fear.
Now all sing together, a jubilant theme,
For a happy old bear loves the song of the stream.

The Brave Little Hedgehog

A hedgehog named Harry was tiny but spry,
He dreamed of adventures, beneath the wide sky.
With a backpack of snacks and a sparkle in eye,
He set out to conquer, determined to fly.

Through fields full of daisies and thickets so thick,
He battled a shadow, a monster—a stick!
With every brave puff, he stood firm and proud,
While friends in the bushes cheered loud in the crowd.

"Come join me, dear pals!" he called with delight,
As he danced on the path, through the day and the night.
The rabbits all chuckled, the birds swooped and swirled,
For the bravest of hearts lived in this small world.

With laughter as fuel and spirits so high,
Harry led his pals, under the same sky.
Together they ventured, through fun-filled terrain,
In the heart of their laughter, joy will remain.

The Mischievous Squirrel's Quest

Squeaky tail and nutty dreams,
A little squirrel plots no seams.
With acorn caps and friends in tow,
They plan to steal a seedling show.

They scurry past the barking hound,
With giggles echoing around.
A flip and flop—a daring trick,
Success! They snagged the biggest pick!

But wait! A glance from up above,
A hawk swoops down, no time for love.
With frantic leaps they dart away,
Through branches high, they dance and sway.

At dusk, they share their story bold,
Of daring deeds and treasure gold.
With laughter loud, they make a pact,
For more wild quests—this fun's a fact.

The Tale of Two Shadows

Two shadows danced upon the wall,
Each one claiming to be tall.
One said, "Look! I catch the light!"
The other giggled, "Not tonight!"

They argued shades of dark and bright,
As night rolled in with a playful bite.
One stretched long to touch the floor,
While the other chuckled, "I'll be more!"

A tussle there, a push and shove,
Each shadow shouted, "I am glove!"
Together they formed a comical sight,
A jumble of dark, a mix of light.

By dawn they laughed, their feud gave way,
In sunlight bright, no more to play.
They twirled together, side by side,
Two shadows merging, fun their guide.

Echoes in the Ancient Bark

In ancient trees where whispers dwell,
A woodpecker taps a silly spell.
Each knock and drum brings life anew,
As squirrels giggle, it's their cue.

They gather 'round the gnarled trunk,
Listening close to the old wood's funk.
With mossy giggles, they take their turn,
In the echoes, they twist and churn.

A fox pops in with wily grin,
"What tales do you share, where to begin?"
The trees reply with crackling cheer,
"Join us in laughter, come right here!"

As sunbeams filter through the leaves,
The laughter swells like autumn eves.
With echoes bright, they dance around,
In ancient bark, the joy is found.

Where Moonlight Dances

In a grove where shadows prance,
The moonlight twirls, it takes a chance.
Crickets chirp and fireflies wink,
In this twilight, no time to think.

A raccoon rolls in silver beams,
Wearing dreams stitched with moonlit seams.
He trips and slips, oh what a sight!
The stars above begin to light.

With laughter shared among the crew,
Each night they build their stories new.
A dance-off starts, it's wild and free,
With moonlight laughing in harmony.

At dawn they leave, their mirth remains,
In every leaf, in all terrains.
Where moonlight danced on playful nights,
The world awakens with their delights.

Shadows of the Sagebrush Satire

In the sagebrush, a rabbit pranced,
Wearing glasses, it seemed entranced.
A coyote laughed, with a toothy grin,
"You're as wise as a fox on a whim!"

The tortoise joked, moving quite slow,
"It's not the speed, but the wit that will glow!"
The hare just winked, with a playful twitch,
"Let's race to the moon, what a glorious hitch!"

Sagebrush swayed to a rhythm unheard,
As frogs croaked tunes, squawking their word.
A dance of mischief beneath the bright moon,
In shadows where wisdom and folly commune.

So laugh along with the critters at night,
In the sagebrush land, everything's light.
With a twitch of the ear, and a sly little grin,
Go join the fun, let the adventure begin!

Adventures on the Forest Floor

On the forest floor, a squirrel found cheese,
With a gleam in his eye and a buzz in the breeze.
He gathered pals, each ready to snack,
A feasting roster, no room for lack!

A wise old owl watched from his tree,
"Don't tell the mouse, he'll cause a big spree!"
But the mouse heard whispers of the great cheese,
And dashed to the party with remarkable ease!

Chasing the crumbs, through leaves they scurried,
Each friend for themselves, no one too hurried.
The laughter rang out, as vines twirled tight,
In the ruckus and fun that lit up the night!

The forest was filled with a magical cheer,
As critters danced round, spreading joy far and near.
They feasted on laughter, and friendship so pure,
In this charming realm, where adventures endure.

Songs of the Spindly Stalks

Amongst the spindly stalks, a party would start,
With wobbly daisies each playing their part.
A ladybug sang, with a voice full of cheer,
"Join in, dear friends, the fun's drawing near!"

The wind joined the dance, with a whimsical twist,
Caressing the flowers, ensuring no mist.
The grass hummed a tune, swaying to and fro,
As crickets auditioned for the late-night show!

The moonlight giggled, as it painted the scene,
While the owls hooted softly, quite serene.
Each creature at play, in the night so alive,
Creating a symphony, where laughter will thrive.

So waltz with the weeds, and sway with the trees,
In the realm of the stalks, do what you please.
In a world full of joy, let your spirit take flight,
As the songs of the spindly stalks fill the night.

Mysteries of the Meadow Musings

In the meadow of musings, a hen pecked around,
Clucking of secrets, of laughter profound.
A cow shared a story, grand and quite bold,
Of a mouse with a crown, who was shy but not cold.

The butterflies flittered, all colors in tow,
Whispering legends, as they danced to and fro.
A puddle reflected the joy and surprise,
As the hen cackled tales of the skies.

A turtle, quite wise, offered up sage,
"What fun is a fable locked up in a cage?"
And the creatures all nodded, in agreement so sweet,
As they promised to share their musical beat.

So gather your friends, let the musings unfold,
For in the meadow's heart, lies adventures untold.
With laughter and stories intertwining their fates,
In this whimsical realm, they'll open the gates.

A Festival of Flickering Lanterns

In the night, lanterns sway,
With giggles lighting the way.
Glowbugs dance, a comic crew,
Winking bright as they fly through.

A cat in a bowtie prances,
While a frog joins in the dances.
Balloons float like silly dreams,
As laughter bursts at the seams.

Marshmallows roast to a tune,
Underneath the silly moon.
The night is filled with delight,
As shadows play in the light.

So join the fun, raise a cheer,
For every chuckle brings us near.
With flickering joy all around,
In this glow, true joy is found.

Shadows of the Singing Sedge

In a garden filled with cheer,
Singing sedges draw us near.
With whispers that tickle the night,
Their melodies bring pure delight.

A duck in a top hat struts,
While a squirrel plays around with nuts.
The shadows dance, a playful sight,
As laughter twirls in full flight.

Mice in bowties join the show,
Swaying gently to and fro.
With squeaks that echo all around,
In this tune, joy is unbound.

Under stars, they take a bow,
A whimsical performance, somehow.
So join the revels, sing along,
Where shadows weave the heart's sweet song.

The Legend of the Radiant Roots

In a field where bright roots grow,
There's a rumor that we all know.
They tickle toes and laugh with glee,
Spreading joy like a wild sea.

A snail in boots creeps with flair,
While daisies toss their flowery hair.
The roots hum a silly song,
Inviting all to sing along.

A dance-off starts, the critters cheer,
With every groove, they draw near.
From bunnies to turtles in a line,
Spreading giggles that intertwine.

Legends speak of this delight,
Where roots burst into laughter at night.
So come and join this playful spree,
Where even plants dance joyfully.

Mysteries of the Midnight Meadow

In the meadow where moonbeams play,
Mischief blooms in a cheeky way.
Fireflies wink like tiny stars,
As crickets strum on their guitars.

A cow in disguise, oh what a sight,
Wears glasses crooked, a true delight.
With dancing sheep and owls that hoot,
Each moment's wrapped in playful loot.

The roses giggle with the breeze,
As rabbits bounce and tease with ease.
In this meadow full of cheer,
Giggles echo loud and clear.

Midnight revels, wild and free,
In this land of jubilee.
So come, enchanted, take your stand,
And feel the joy of this merry land.

Where Squirrels Sing and Shadows Play

In the heart of a tree, where the critters convene,
Squirrels juggle acorns, a comical scene.
With tails all a-twirl, they leap with delight,
Chasing their shadows, they dance through the night.

A badger in bowtie tries to conduct,
While rabbits in top hats perform with great luck.
The folly unfolds under moonlight's embrace,
As giggles and chortles fill up the whole space.

The owls hoot applause, they twinkle their eyes,
While fireflies twirl in a luminous guise.
In this raucous retreat, joy knows no end,
Where laughter erupts, and all critters blend.

So if ever you wander through thickets and trees,
Join the merry party, let go and feel free.
For in the woods whisper secrets galore,
Where squirrels sing sweetly, and shadows implore.

Legends Woven in Moss

Beneath the old oak, where legends are spun,
Moss tells of the mischief of everyone.
The pixies in twirls, they sprinkle their cheer,
With giggles and whispers that only we hear.

A fox in a cape claims to fly to the stars,
While rabbits debate the best cheese for their bars.
They share silly tales of adventures afar,
In the warmth of the glow, beneath twilight's guitar.

With leaves as confetti, they crown the night king,
To reign with a jester who's never quite king.
The beams dance along, weaving magic so fine,
In a world full of wonder, where laughter aligns.

So lie on the moss where the stories take flight,
Feel the pulse of the woodland, embrace the delight.
For even the woodpecker joins in the fun,
As legends wrap round us, till the day's finally done.

The Magic of the Timberland

In the timberland thick, the trees wear a grin,
A wise old raccoon knows where to begin.
With trickster's delight, he shares his best brew,
Of blossoms and laughter, a whimsical stew.

The porcupines waddle in pajamas so bright,
While squirrels play tag till the blanketing night.
With pinecone balloons, sort of silly and grand,
They host a grand party, all holding a hand.

The whispers of leaves tell jokes from the roots,
As chipmunks juggle berries, their sweetest pursuits.
The magic ignites in the glow of the moon,
Where friendship and laughter make merriment bloom.

So come join the fun, where the wild critters stay,
In the heart of the timber, where joy finds its way.
For here, every moment is spun into gold,
A tale of pure magic that never grows old.

Echoes of Elixirs and Elms

In the shade of the elms, a brew pot does bubble,
Where bats brew their potions, creating some trouble.
A wise old turtle stirs, with a wink and a nod,
While critters tiptoe, enchanted, awed.

The squirrel adds honey, a dash of sweet charm,
While hedgehogs roll in, adding quills to disarm.
With laughter and giggles, they gather around,
As the elixir of joy slowly warms the ground.

The fairies bring glowworms, to light up the night,
While bees serenade with songs in polite.
In a world overflowing with joy and delight,
Their spirits unite under stars shining bright.

So raise up your cups to the magic we chase,
For echoes and laughter completely embrace.
In the land of the elms, let the wonders unfold,
As we share in the stories that never grow old.

The Great Gather of the Forest Folk

In a glade where the tall trees sway,
The critters come out to laugh and play.
A squirrel juggles acorns with flair,
While rabbits join in with style and care.

Bears bring honey, sweet and bold,
While badgers spin yarns from days of old.
The owls hoot jokes that go way past dark,
And frogs hop along, a comical lark.

With mushrooms as stools and leaves as plates,
They feast on giggles and share their fates.
The wind whispers tales of tricks on the way,
As evening falls, they shout, "Hooray!"

Under stars, the forest sings bright,
A wild merry dance, a joyous sight.
Friendship blooms in the crisp night air,
In the great gather, there's fun to spare.

The Maple's Melody

A maple tree stood tall and grand,
With leaves a-twirl like a marching band.
It played a tune in the gentle breeze,
As squirrels danced round with agile ease.

A chipmunk hummed, a tune so spry,
While butterflies fluttered, oh so high.
Each note a giggle, each chord a laugh,
As forest folk joined this silly gaffe.

The branches swayed, a natural drum,
With woodpeckers tapping, a catchy thrum.
Bouncing berries added to the score,
Creating a symphony that none could ignore.

With laughter and song echoing through,
The maple tree swayed as if it knew.
In this merry moment, fun was the key,
A melody danced through the forest like glee.

The Mischievous Moss

In the shadowed nook of a grand oak tree,
Lived a mossy fellow as spry as can be.
With sneaky tricks and a cheeky grin,
He loved to play games, let the fun begin!

He'd tickle the toes of the unsuspecting,
And whisper soft secrets that had them connecting.
A race of the snails, a crawl through the dew,
Gathered all dwellers for fun anew.

He rolled with the breeze, light as a feather,
Creating ruckus, binding them together.
With laughter that rang from bough to bough,
The forest resounded with joy in the now.

As shadows deepened and day turned to night,
Moss curled up, content with his delight.
For in every giggle, under skies so vast,
The mischievous moss made memories last.

A Dance of Dandelions

In a field where the sunflowers sway,
Dandelions gathered for a whimsical play.
With tiny hats made of petals bright,
They spun and twirled, a glorious sight.

The breeze joined in with a soft humming tune,
While ladybugs waltzed beneath the moon.
Each puff ball giggled in the warm sun's glow,
As laughter erupted from the flowers below.

They leapt like fairies, carefree and spry,
Under the watchful gaze of the sky.
With seeds all afloat, a magical turn,
As each little dancer took flight and would churn.

In this riot of color, a story was spun,
Of dandelion charm and a race to have fun.
So when you see them swirl in the air,
Remember their dance, full of joy and care.

The Fox and the Fragrant Flowers

In a garden bright with hues,
A crafty fox sought lively views.
He sniffed the blooms, oh how they danced,
His nose twitched twice, in a happy trance.

But as he pranced, with charm and grace,
He tripped on vines, oh what a chase!
The flowers laughed, a joyful crew,
As the fox rolled in with a vibrant hue.

With petals stuck upon his tail,
He plotted schemes that would not fail.
Yet every plan turned to a joke,
As each new step caused roots to poke.

In the end, with laughter loud,
The fox embraced the blooming crowd.
He learned that fun was in the tangle,
No need for schemes—just let them dangle.

The Owl's Wisdom

A wise old owl sat high on a tree,
Wrapped in thoughts so wondrously free.
Each night he spoke with quite a flair,
Sharing wisdom like a bold millionaire.

He saw the squirrel, in a frantic whirl,
Gathering acorns, in quite a twirl.
"Oh dear friend, you look so stressed!"
The squirrel laughed, saying, "I jest!"

With a wink, the owl replied with glee,
"Remember, buddy, just let it be."
But the squirrel grinned, and said, "I can't,
These nuts won't gather themselves, they shan't!"

And so they danced under the moon's soft glow,
The wise old owl, and the squirrel in tow.
Chasing shadows, they forgot their fuss,
In the night's embrace, they found their trust.

Tapestry of Twisting Vines

In a garden of vines that twisted high,
A chameleon played tag, oh my oh my!
With colors bright, it sought to blend,
But each new twist met a silly end.

He chased a butterfly with flared delight,
But tangled his tail in a comical plight.
The vines chuckled, swaying to the beat,
As the chameleon did a silly repeat.

"Be still, dear friend, you're spinning too fast!"
Said a wise old tortoise as he passed.
"A dance of grace in those leaves so fine,
Might just help you untwist and shine!"

With newfound moves, he spun and swayed,
The tapestry vibrant, never frayed.
In laughter echoed, a whimsical tune,
As vines wrapped round, beneath the moon.

The Quest for the Golden Nut

A zealot squirrel sought a nut so rare,
With fur ablaze, he sped with flair.
Through forests deep and hills so steep,
He laughed aloud, "This prize I'll keep!"

He asked the rabbit, "Have you seen?
The golden nut? It's fit for a queen!"
The rabbit snickered, "Oh what a quest!
But nuts are nuts; just like the rest!"

Undeterred, he danced through trees,
With acorns dropping like a playful breeze.
He tumbled and bumbled, full of cheer,
As every critter gathered near.

At last, he spied, beneath a sun's beam,
A shiny acorn, a wondrous dream.
But as he reached, a gust blew strong,
And off it rolled, with laughter long!

An Acorn's Adventure

An acorn rolled down a forest slope,
Chasing a squirrel with a grand, wild hope.
"Catch me if you can!" it shouted with glee,
While dodging roots like a sprightly spree.

It bounced past mushrooms with a comical spin,
Near the bubbling brook where the frogs liked to grin.
"I'm a mighty oak!" it proclaimed with delight,
Follow me, friends, to a fun-filled night.

The squirrel just chuckled, eyes wide with surprise,
As the acorn danced under the big summer skies.
With a flip and a flop, it tumbled around,
Creating a joy that simply astounds.

Alas! A badger took the race as a dare,
Chasing the acorn with a comical flair.
In the heart of the woods, laughter did bloom,
As nature's great stage filled the darkening room.

The Lure of Luminous Fireflies

In a glade lit by stars, with a giggle and gleeful,
Fireflies twinkled like laughter, so whimsical and peaceful.
"Catch me!" they buzzed, with a flicker and flash,
Dancing on whispers, a luminous splash.

Little Tommy the toad watched with glee,
As the fireflies circled, a whimsical spree.
He tried to leap high, but he landed with plop,
And the fireflies giggled, then twinkled and stopped.

From bushes and brambles, they soared up enthralled,
Playing hide and seek, as the night softly called.
With a wink and a wink, they sparked pure delight,
Nature's giggles embraced in the night.

Soon a breeze fluttered, and a charm it did weave,
As laughter erupted, the night would believe.
In the tails of the fireflies, a joke most divine,
In the glow of the moment, all hearts intertwined.

The Oak Tree's Tale

Under the skies where the breezes sing,
An oak tree chuckled, imagining spring.
"I've watched little critters, oh what a spree!"
Its branches held stories, as wide as the sea.

A rabbit once danced on a twig that was low,
But tripped on a root and fell down with a 'whoa!'
The oak let out laughter, its leaves all a-sway,
As the rabbit jumped up, still ready to play.

A raccoon with mischief decided to climb,
In the search for a snack, oh the silliest crime!
He stumbled and fumbled, the acorns fell down,
Creating a shower that looked like a crown.

"Life's full of giggles!" the oak tree sighed,
As a squirrel swung by, with the grace of a glide.
With a rustle of leaves and a chuckle so bright,
The tales of the oak filled the heart with delight.

The Magic of Midsummer Nights

On midsummer nights when the moon's shining bright,
Creatures came out for a whimsical flight.
With laughter that echoed, they danced in a ring,
A gathering of joy, where the critters would sing.

A hedgehog named Harry wore a hat much too big,
He tripped on his feet, did a rolly-polly jig.
The owls hooted loudly, their eyes wide with cheer,
As they watched all the antics with soft, gentle peering.

Fireflies swirled round like a round ballet,
Lighting up paths for the creatures at play.
With the chirp of the crickets as music so sweet,
Midsummer nights held magic, impossible to beat.

So gather your friends, let the fun take its flight,
In the glow of the stars, until dawn's early light.
With giggles and dances, the memories ignite,
In the heart of the night, everything feels right.

Chronicles of the Canopied Kingdom

In a kingdom high, where the squirrels chatter,
A raccoon dressed fine, in a coat that won't flatter.
He prances and twirls, with a grin on his face,
While birds giggle softly, watching his race.

A frog in a crown, perched upon a high tree,
Croaking his laws, oh-so-merrily.
The ants throw a party, complete with a feast,
Where each tiny dancer is a jolly little beast.

The owls tell tales, wrapped in moonlight's glow,
Of a fox who would sing, with a voice made of snow.
They laugh till they cry, under starlit delight,
In the canopied realm, everything feels right.

With laughter like raindrops, they dance through the night,

A circus of critters, in pure forest flight.
In this joyous place, every creature is grand,
Sharing mischief and dreams, across the broad land.

Joys Among the Branches

In the canopy's joy, where the sunlight will play,
Monkeys swing swiftly, like it's their birthday.
They toss ripe bananas, a slippery game,
Each splat on a fox brings more giggles and fame.

The wise old blue jay, with tales so absurd,
Spins stories of frogs who laughed like a bird.
While underneath, mushrooms all dance in a row,
Tickled by breezes that make them all glow.

A turtle on roller skates glides with a cheer,
Zipping past shadows, he's the star of the year.
Rabbits throw carrots like confetti in flight,
Declaring their laughter, the talk of the night.

These joys of the branches, where fun never ends,
Fill days with giggles and laughter, my friends.
In a world full of whimsy, both strange and divine,
Among all the branches, the fun will entwine.

The Mirth of the Misty Woods

In the misty woods where the whispers reside,
A bear wore a hat, and he couldn't decide.
To eat or to dance, both options seemed sweet,
So he joined in a jig, on two very full feet.

The rabbits convene, a council of jest,
Debating what snacks they consider the best.
With popcorn and berries, they create a big mess,
Amid laughter and giggles, their worries regress.

A hedgehog with charm pulls a prank, oh so sly,
Sneezing a tune, oh my, oh my!
The deer roll their eyes, but can't help but join,
As mirth fills the air like a sweet, joyous coin.

Through the misty woods, where the mischief is grand,
Creatures conspire, with magic unplanned.
In this world of laughter, both silly and wise,
The joy of the forest is seen through its eyes.

Fables of Forest Friends

In the heart of the woods, where the laughter is loud,
A rabbit made muffins and gathered a crowd.
The hedgehogs all danced on a plate made of pie,
While chipmunks recited a jingle to try.

A wise old owl hooted, "What's all this fuss?"
As badgers in bow ties engaged in a bus.
They drove it around on the forest floor's route,
Laughing and jiving, all in funny suits.

The laughter rang out as they sang in the sun,
Bouncing and tumbling, oh what silly fun!
A fox played the drums, the beat oh so fine,
While critters all rallied with nuts and with wine.

With each little story, the joy only grows,
In the realm of the trees, where the friendship glows.
These tales of togetherness, cheeky and bright,
In a world of soft humor, the heart takes delight.

Guardians of the Greenery

In the heart of the glen, where the giggles reside,
A squirrel wore glasses, quite full of pride.
He reads his fine book on a branch so tall,
While raccoons debate the best nuts of all.

Beneath the tall pine, the owl takes a nap,
Counting those critters who'll fall in a trap.
But who could resist, when the sun shines so bright?
They dance and they prance till the fall of the night.

The bunnies perform with their delightful cheer,
Sprinkling the meadow with joy far and near.
A frog cracks a joke from his lily pad throne,
And laughter erupts through the forest alone.

So gather, dear friends, in this whimsical place,
Where each silly creature brings smiles to your face.
In the guardians' realm, where the humor runs free,
Nature's a stage for you and for me!

The Timeless Tangle

In a woods full of twists, where the branches all weave,
A chicken tried dancing, but she'd misjudge her cleave.
With a flap and a flop, she stumbled around,
While the rabbits just chuckled, falling to ground.

The hedgehog was spinning, dressed up like a star,
With sequins and glitter, oh, he raised the bar!
But tripped on a twig, what a sight to behold,
He rolled down the hill, quite theatrical and bold.

Amidst all the tangle, the laughter did swell,
For each quirky creature had stories to tell.
From prancing to twirling, it was quite the show,
In the timeless tangle, where smiles freely flow.

So join in the fun, let your worries unfasten,
In the world of the wild, where the mirth is a-castin'.
With each little tumble, every slip and each fall,
You'll find joy in the chaos, a choice to stand tall!

The Faery in the Ferns

In emerald ferns where the faery does twirl,
She giggles and dances, her hair in a whirl.
With a flick of her wand, she sprinkles the dew,
Making daisies giggle, as if they just knew.

A mouse in a waistcoat joins in the delight,
He somersaults 'round, quite a marvelous sight.
Then whispers to flowers, "What's the latest news?"
And they rustle and reply with a flurry of hues.

The fireflies gather, their lights start to blink,
In a flash mob of laughter, they shimmer and wink.
While crickets compose a symphony sweet,
Nature's own orchestra, a rhythm discreet.

So wander with whimsy through glades filled with fun,
Where faeries and critters share joy 'neath the sun.
In the world of the whimsical, silliness reigns,
As life in the ferny glens forever entertains!

The Rhapsody of the Rustling Leaves

The leaves start to chatter, a gossiping crew,
As wind plays with whispers, it tickles them too.
A fox in a scarf joins the ecological jest,
Telling tall tales of the critters' big quest.

A hedgehog serenades, with a tune that's so grand,
While mice tap their feet, arranging a band.
"Oh, gather around!" says the wise old tree,
"For stories of laughter will set all hearts free!"

The brook sings along with its burbling tune,
As fireflies dance under the light of the moon.
The orchestra plays, though it seems quite absurd,
For each little sound is a joyful word.

So linger in laughter, let merriment rise,
In a rhapsody woven with giggles and sighs.
This forest of friends with their sounds and their glee,
Will fill even grumpies with sparkle and spree!

The Wandering Willows

Once there were willows, so sly and so spry,
They danced in the breeze, reaching low and high.
They whispered sweet secrets to bugs passing by,
And laughed as the squirrels fell out of the sky.

They'd bend and they'd sway, take a bow to the moon,
While frogs riding bicycles sang a cute tune.
The owls hooted jokes, oh, they made quite the ruckus,
As fireflies twinkled, saying, 'Join our circus!'

The willows grew tired of the same old old song,
So they devised mischief, both clever and strong.
With giggles and grins, they plotted at dusk,
They played hide and seek with a mischievous musk.

So if you hear laughter, just follow the sound,
To find those sweet willows, where giggles abound.
Be careful, dear friend, and wear the right shoes,
Or you might just trip over their playful ruse.

The Serpent of the Silvery Stream

In a stream ever glimmering, a serpent was sly,
With scales made of silver and a glint in his eye.
He danced through the water with fanciful flair,
Making fish giggle, swimming without a care.

His favorite pastime? A game of charades,
With turtles who dabbled in whimsical trades.
They'd act out the shadows and splash with delight,
While dragonflies darted, all buzzing with light.

But when otters appeared, claiming all the fun,
The serpent swirled round, saying, "I'm not quite done!"
He leaped with a twist, and a wiggle, a whirl,
And fell for a moment, a great sandy swirl.

Those otters just chuckled, they couldn't resist,
As the serpent came up, all soggy and kissed.
With laughter a-washing, they splished and they splashed,

In the silvery stream, where the joy ever crashed.

The Tale of the Tricky Toad

There lived a fine toad with a glimmering crown,
He'd hop and he'd skip, never wearing a frown.
With a wink and a smile, he'd pull sneaky tricks,
On all of the critters, his good friends and picks.

He'd hide in the mud, call it muck-tastic fun,
Then leap with a splash, laughing, "Now, look what I've done!"
The rabbits would yelp, while the hedgehogs all giggled,
As the toad chortled loudly, their hearts always wiggled.

One day with a cheer, he challenged a frog,
"To race through the reeds, don't you dare be a slog!"
But slippery paths led to quite the surprise,
As they both lost their grip and fell under the skies.

With muddy green coats and a wide silly grin,
They laughed at their mess, felt the joy deep within.
In the sun-soaked marsh, where the fun never wanes,
The tricky old toad never quite feels the pains.

The Lullaby of the Leafy Kingdom

In a kingdom of leaves, where the laughter would grow,
The little ones giggled, and the wind whispered low.
With dreams made of sunlight and hopes made of cheer,
The night sang a lullaby, soft in the ear.

The foxes would firefly dance on the green,
While badgers and bunnies rehearsed quite the scene.
The stars twinkled softly, like laughter of sprites,
As the creatures were wrapped in their blissful nights.

A chorus of crickets played sweet on the grass,
While owls winked in rhythm, the moon took a pass.
With dreams full of fun, each critter would sway,
To the lullaby's beat, whisking troubles away.

So snug in their nests, in the leafy embrace,
Each creature found peace in the night's gentle grace.
Tomorrow would bring all the games, loud and bright,
But for now, let them dream in the hush of the night.

Secrets Beneath the Evergreens

In the shade where squirrels dance,
A gnome spins tales of chance.
Whispers of secrets soft and sly,
Where shadows chuckle and butterflies fly.

Ticklish roots in a playful twirl,
A bunny hops, giving a whirl.
Underneath the towering trees,
Laughter echoes upon the breeze.

Mice in capes on acorn quests,
Chasing dreams of silly tests.
Acorns tumble with each laughter,
Adventures waiting ever after.

So come and listen, lend an ear,
To tales of joy that bring us cheer.
In nature's giggle, magic we find,
Beneath the pines, love's intertwined.

A Riddle in the Roots

Amidst the roots where mischief grows,
A riddle spins in hushed prose.
What dances on the breeze so light,
In shadows thick, yet out of sight?

A wise old owl perched on high,
Cracks the code with a wink and sigh.
Said the acorn, small yet brave,
"In laughter's heart, true treasures save."

Foxes gather, hats askew,
Playing games with a colorful crew.
Each clue a giggle, each turn a twist,
In the land of laughter, we coexist.

So ponder deeply, young and old,
The secrets among stories told.
For in the roots where riddles play,
Life's silly dance will lead the way.

The Enchanted Acorn

An acorn dreams of skies so bright,
Sprouting wings to take its flight.
With giggling winds that spin and swirl,
It dances 'round in a merry whirl.

Beneath the oak, the critters cheer,
As magic spreads from far and near.
The acorn sings a merry tune,
While sunbeams shimmy 'neath the moon.

Squirrels in capes, they take the stage,
Telling tales of every age.
With each new trick and silly jest,
The forest joins, they're laughing best.

A jump, a twirl, a sudden glide,
The acorn spreads its joy with pride.
In every branch, a story springs,
In nature's heart, the laughter sings.

Legends of the Leafy Grove

In the grove where shadows play,
Legends twinkle bright as day.
A raccoon with a treasure map,
Chasing giggles, not a trap.

Leaves whisper rumors, sharp and sweet,
Of dancing trees and wayward feet.
The tallest birch with laughter loud,
Claims the secrets of the crowd.

Dancing mushrooms in a line,
Underneath the trees, they shine.
Join the tale, don't be shy,
Find the magic in each sigh.

So take a peek and lend an ear,
In leafy tales, there's much to cheer.
For every corner holds a jest,
In playful woods, you're truly blessed.

Whispers of Woodland Wonders

In the glade, a squirrel danced,
Chasing shadows, he pranced.
With acorns as his prized delight,
He juggled them, oh what a sight!

A rabbit giggled, jumps in delight,
While fireflies twinkled in flight.
Mice offered cheese as their cheer,
A woodland party; they all drew near!

The owl hooted with a wink,
'You call that music? I think!'
The frog croaked, his voice so grand,
The rhythm echoed, oh how it spanned!

Amid the fun, laughter would bloom,
As nature's stage filled with room.
And when the night began to fall,
They shared their tales, enchanting all!

Secrets Beneath the Evergreen Canopy

Beneath the boughs, a secret spread,
Of chipmunk wed to a bed of bread.
A sneaky crow, with mischief in tow,
Swapped his shiny pearls for dough!

The wind tickled leaves, a silent giggle,
As hedgehogs danced in a wiggly wiggle.
With mushrooms serving, oh what a feast,
A cabbage roll for every beast!

Grasshoppers laughed, their legs kept springing,
Each note played, the happy birds singing.
The wise old trees, with branches so wide,
Shared whispers of laughter, mysteries to bide.

As sunlight winked through every hue,
They played till shadows had started to brew.
In their world, where fun knows no end,
Every creature, a cherished friend!

Tales of Treetop Treasures

Up high, where the breezes roam,
A mischievous raccoon made a home.
With shiny spoons and a hat made of leaves,
He crafted tales that nobody believes!

The birds perched nearby, in gossip did dwell,
As whispers of treasure passed through the swell.
A squirrel heard and set off on a quest,
To find the prize, he put skills to the test!

A glittering stone? Or maybe a crown?
His imagination spun him around.
Through branches wide, down a slippery slope,
He laughed with delight, fueled by his hope!

At day's end, when the sun turned to gold,
They shared their stories, each one retold.
With treasures of laughter and joy in the air,
In the treetops, friends gathered to share!

Mischief in the Leafy Grove

In the leafy grove, where shadows play,
A cheeky raccoon planned for the day.
He set up traps with sprinkling seeds,
Bait for the birds, oh, it succeeds!

A wise old owl watched from above,
Chuckling softly, feeling the love.
The fox joined in, with a wink and a nod,
'Let's stir up some fun, it won't be odd!'

Together they danced, masked in delight,
Creating a ruckus, oh what a sight!
The other critters, drawn in a flurry,
Joined the fun, forgetting their worry.

As twilight carpeted the grove with stars,
They reveled in joy, forgot all their scars.
In laughter they found their mischievous schemes,
Binding their hearts with the sweetest of dreams!

www.ingramcontent.com/pod-product-compliance
Lightning Source LLC
Chambersburg PA
CBHW071840160426
43209CB00003B/364